DIERCKE GEOGRAPHY

BILINGUALES MODUL FÜR DEN GEOGRAPHIEUNTERRICHT

USA

INTERMEDIATE LEVEL

Moderation:
Prof. Dr. Reinhard Hoffmann

Autoren:
Matthew Appleby
Volker Friedrich
Dieter Haupt
Reinhard Hoffmann
Dirk Reischauer
Dimo M. Rischke

unter Mitwirkung der
Verlagsredaktion

westermann

Cover: Golden Gate Bridge, San Francisco, California

westermann GRUPPE

© 2010 Bildungshaus Schulbuchverlage
Westermann Schroedel Diesterweg Schöningh Winklers GmbH, Braunschweig
www.westermann.de

Druck A^5 / Jahr 2017
Alle Drucke der Serie A sind im Unterricht parallel verwendbar.

Verlagslektorat: Lars Büttner
Umschlaggestaltung und Layout: Thomas Schröder
Druck und Bindung: westermann druck GmbH, Braunschweig

ISBN 978-3-14-**114015**-6

Audiodateien:

DG_M1-004
www.diercke.com

Webcode: Er führt zu den frei zugänglichen Audiodateien im Internet (Vertonung Key terms / Vokabelhilfen).

Textvertonung: Diese Audiodateien sind Teil der Lehrermaterialien, zu denen auch die Lösungen gehören. Ausgewählte Texte des Moduls werden von einem Muttersprachler vorgelesen.

Arbeitshinweise

Dieses bilinguale Modul ist zweigeteilt; erkennbar am Farbleitsystem: Auf den *Topical Pages* (Themenseiten, gelb) findest du das geographische Fachwissen. Die *Practical Pages* (grün) bieten dir im zweiten Teil für die einzelnen Themenseiten praktische Übungen an.

Das Modul unterstützt dich durch sprachliche Hilfestellungen aktiv bei der Arbeit im englischsprachigen Geographieunterricht:

1. Vokabelhilfen – Übersetzungen
Bestimmte englische Begriffe sind mit einem Übersetzungshinweis versehen. Mithilfe der Indexzahlen kannst du die Übersetzungen schnell finden. Sie befinden sich am unteren Seitenrand. Die Reihenfolge der Indexzahlen folgt zunächst dem Text und dann den Abbildungen.

2. Box: Helpful words and phrases
Diese Boxen bieten dir hilfreiche Wortvorschläge und Redewendungen an. Sie sind vor allem wertvoll, wenn du auf Englisch etwas beschreiben oder erklären sollst. Alle Boxen verweisen dich darauf, wo sie dir helfen können (eine bestimmte Aufgabe, ein bestimmtes Material).

3. Box: Hinweise für ...
Diese Boxen bieten zusätzliche Übersetzungshilfen oder andere Hinweise in deutscher Sprache.

4. Box: Key terms / Glossary
Key terms sind wichtige Fachbegriffe. Du findest sie auf jeder Seite aufgelistet in einer Box. Jeder Key term ist im *Glossar* am Ende des Moduls nachschlagbar. Dort findest du eine Lautschrift, welche dir die richtige Aussprache zeigt, sowie, wenn notwendig, eine englische Definition.

5. Toolkitverweis
pp. 8–9
Photographs

Das *Diercke Geography Toolkit* ist eine „Werkzeugbox" für den bilingualen Geographieunterricht. Wenn du darauf zurückgreifen kannst, dann nutze dieses Symbol. Es weist darauf hin, wenn das Toolkit dir helfen kann und zeigt dir auch gleich die Seiten, auf denen du nachschlagen musst.

Contrasting Nature – Relief

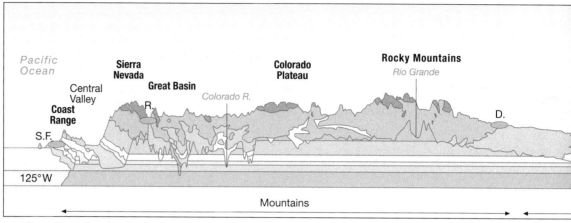

M1 Cross section[1] of North America

pp. 8–9
Photographs

M2 Californian Central Valley

The West is dominated by mountain ranges[2] and valleys, which run in a north-south direction from Alaska to Mexico.

In Central Valley lettuce[3] fields are irrigated in the middle of summer. Water is needed during the dry and warm summers. The winters are mild and wet.

M3 Great Salt Lake

On the upland plateaus[4] of the Great Basin[5] in the mountainous west there is a continental climate with hot and dry summers and cold and dry winters.

The shores[6] of the Great Salt Lake are covered by a thick crust of salt in summer, when the water level is low.

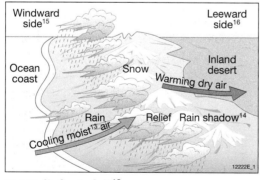

M4 Relief rainfall[12]

M5 Climate data from east to west

City	Height above sea level	Precipitation per year	Average temperature
Atlantic City	3 m	1075 mm	12.3 °C
Indianapolis	241 m	996 mm	11.2 °C
Kansas City	365 m	947 mm	12.8 °C
Denver	1610 m	380 mm	10.2 °C
Reno	1342 m	180 mm	9.4 °C
San Francisco	62 m	670 mm	13.8 °C

[1] cross section – *Querschnitt*
[2] mountain range – *Bergkette*
[3] lettuce – *Kopfsalat*
[4] upland plateau – *Hochlandplateau*

[5] basin – *Becken*
[6] shore – *Küstenlinie*

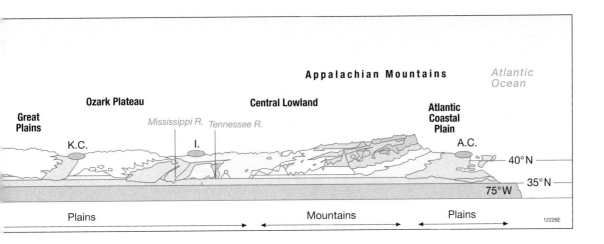

Appalachian Mountains

Atlantic Ocean

Ozark Plateau

Central Lowland

Great Plains

Atlantic Coastal Plain

Mississippi R.   Tennessee R.

K.C.   I.   A.C.

40°N

35°N

75°W

Plains   Mountains   Plains

12226E

M6 Great Plains

East of the Rocky Mountains there are the lowland plains[7] and plateaus.

Before the Europeans came to America, large herds of bison lived on the dry and almost completely flat prairies.

Today the Great Plains are the largest wheat-[8] producing region in the world.

M7 Coastal Plains

East of the Appalachian Mountains there is a wide coastal plain[9]. The land use varies[10] greatly from north to south.

The White House in Washinghton D.C. may be snow-covered in winter, though it is located[11] as far south as Lisbon and Athens in Europe.

Key terms:

- basin
- coastal plain
- leeward side
- lowland
- plain
- plateau
- rain shadow
- relief
- relief rainfall
- upland
- windward side

Tasks

1 With the help of M1 and your atlas:
a) describe a trip through the USA visiting the cities mentioned in M5 (states, rivers, relief, landscapes) and
b) calculate the length of your trip.

2 Describe the effects of relief rainfall between San Francisco and Reno (M4, M5).

Helpful words and phrases

(for M1, photos, Task 1):

The cross section
... deals with ...
... on the plain ...
... in the mountains ...
... on the plateau ...
... in the basin ...
... in the west ...
in the central part ...
in the east ...

The photograph
... shows ...
... gives information about ...
... in the foreground ...
... in the centre ...
... on the right hand side ...
... on the left hand side ...
... in the background ...

---

[7] lowland plain – *Tieflandebene*
[8] wheat – *Weizen*
[9] coastal plain – *Küstenebene*
[10] vary (to) – *(sich) ändern*
[11] located – *gelegen*

[12] relief rainfall – *Steigungsregen*
[13] moist – *feucht*
[14] rain shadow – *Regenschatten*
[15] windward side – *windzugewandte Seite*
[16] leeward side – *windabgewandte Seite*

Contrasting Nature – Climate and Vegetation

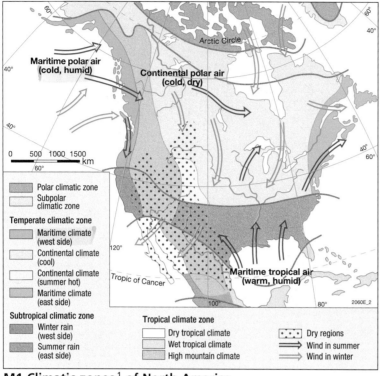

M1 Climatic zones[1] of North America

North America is full of contrasts. From the Arctic tundra in Alaska and northern Canada (M2) to the deserts in Nevada (M5) or the mangrove swamps[2] in Florida (M6) there are many different habitats[3] for plants, animals and humans. Mainly three factors work together to create this natural variety.

Factor one is the temperature: between the icy Arctic Ocean and the warm Gulf of Mexico there is a great difference in temperature. So we find polar bears near the Arctic Circle[4] and alligators near the Tropic of Cancer[5].

More people like to live in the warmer areas (USA, population density[6]: 30 inhabitants/sq km) than in the colder regions (Canada, population density: 3.2 inhabitants/sq km).

Factor two is the precipitation[7]: areas near the Atlantic or Pacific Ocean are relatively moist, the centre of North America is much drier. There are woodlands in the moist coastal regions (M3, M4, and M6). Prairies and deserts[8] (M5) in the dry central regions have no trees. Not many people live in these dry regions, where farming is difficult and water is scarce. The wetter coastal areas, however, are densely populated[9] and, when flat, provide farmland.

Factor three is the height of the land: in the mountains it is colder than in the lowlands. Due to relief rainfall, the windward side has got more precipitation than the leeward side. This is clearly visible in the west, where the winds normally come from the Pacific Ocean. Few people live in the mountainous west with its steep slopes[10], dry inner basins, and plateaus. Most people live in the lower lying plains of the central and coastal regions of the United States.

Tasks

pp. 26–27
Prepare and Give
a Talk

1 What makes the climate in North America so full of contrasts? Prepare a short talk.

pp. 6–7
Thematic Maps

2 Find the five locations (M2–M6) in an atlas and describe the climate and vegetation there.

Key terms:

- boreal
- coniferous forest
- climate (continental, maritime)
- climatic zone (polar, temperate, sub-/tropical)
- desert
- deciduous forest
- mangrove swamp
- precipitation
- temperature
- tundra

---

[1] climatic zone – *Klimazone*
[2] mangrove swamp – *Mangrovensumpf*
[3] habitat – *Lebensraum*
[4] Arctic Circle – *Nördlicher Polarkreis*
[5] Tropic of Cancer – *Nördlicher Wendekreis (Wendekreis des Krebses)*
[6] population density – *Bevölkerungsdichte*
[7] precipitation – *Niederschlag*
[8] desert – *Wüste*
[9] densely populated – *dicht bevölkert*
[10] slope – *Hang*

M2 Tundra in northern Canada

Baker Lake / Canada
4m   64°18'N/96°0'W
°C / mm
T = − 11.9 °C
P = 208 mm
J F M A M J J A S O N D
12331E

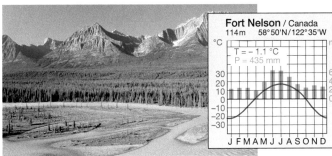

Fort Nelson / Canada
114m   58°50'N/122°35'W
°C / mm
T = − 1.1 °C
P = 435 mm
J F M A M J J A S O N D
12332E

M3 Boreal coniferous forest[11] in central Canada

M4 Temperate deciduous forest[12] in New England

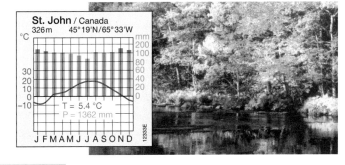

St. John / Canada
326m   45°19'N/65°33'W
°C / mm
T = 5.4 °C
P = 1362 mm
J F M A M J J A S O N D
12333E

Reno / USA
1342m   39°30'N/119°47'W
°C / mm
T = 9.4 °C
P = 180 mm
J F M A M J J A S O N D
12334E

M5 Desert in Nevada

M6 Tropical mangrove swamp in Florida

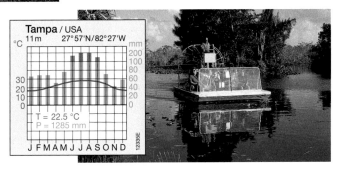

Tampa / USA
11m   27°57'N/82°27'W
°C / mm
T = 22.5 °C
P = 1285 mm
J F M A M J J A S O N D
12335E

Helpful words and phrases
(for Task 1):
There are (different) belts stretching from ... to ...
There is a ... kilometres wide belt ...
From north to south ...
The dry regions are located in ...
The area of the continental climate is ...
The wind directions vary from ... to ...

[11] boreal coniferous forest – *borealer Nadelwald*
[12] temperate deciduous forest – *Laubwald der gemäßigten Zone*

M1 Inland destruction by hurricane 'Katrina' (Louisiana 2005)

Extreme Weather Conditions

Each year many North Americans die due to violent[1] storms such as hurricanes, tornadoes, and blizzards[2]. Today, however, they can be forecasted[3] with the help of satellites and aeroplanes. Weather stations watch the weather all the time. From this data, weather forecasts are made with the fastest computers. People hear the warnings from the programs on TV and radio in time, so they can protect[4] themselves.

Not so long ago, there were no satellites, computers, and television. So hurricanes, blizzards, and tornadoes did more damage[5].

Reasons for violent storms

One of the reasons why Americans are more at risk from strong storms than Europeans is the different order[6] of mountain ranges in Europe and North America.

In Europe, the Alps and Pyrenees stop or slow down cold air masses which try to flow from the north to the Mediterranean Sea. In the other direction, these mountains keep the hot air from Africa away from Central Europe.

In North America there are no north-south barriers[7]. In the East, the Appalachian Moun-

M2 After a blizzard (New York)

M3 Tornado or 'twister' (Texas)

---

[1] violent   –   *sehr stark, heftig*
[2] blizzard   –   *US-Bezeichnung für einen Schneesturm*
[3] forecast (to)   –   *vorhersagen*
[4] protect (to)   –   *schützen*

[5] damage   –   *Schaden*
[6] order   –   *hier: Anordnung*
[7] barrier   –   *Barriere*

tains run[8] in a north-south direction and so do the mountain ranges of the West. So the hot moist air from the Tropics can sometimes travel far north. Cold arctic air, called the 'northers', may damage crops along the Gulf coast in springtime (M4).

Hot, moist air masses have a lot of energy. This energy is set free when cold and warm air masses meet. Tornadoes and blizzards, the violent storms of northern and central North America, are the result.

Blizzards

In blizzards a lot of snow can fall in a very short time, and thus bring life to a standstill[9] (M2).

For example in Silver Lake (Colorado) there were 196 cm of snow in 24 hours. The 'Great Blizzard of 1888' took the lives of 400 people in the North-East.

Tornadoes

The highest wind speed ever recorded inside a tornado was measured in Oklahoma at 318 mph. The suction[10] of such a twister, created by warm rising air meeting cold air, can make houses explode (M3).

The most deadly tornado was the 'Tri-State tornado of 1925'. Though tornadoes normally do not last long, this twister ran through three Mid-West states and killed 695 people. On average[11] there are 800 tornadoes in the USA in one year, most of them in the central and western states.

M5 Road after the flooding caused by hurricane 'Katrina' (Louisiana 2005)

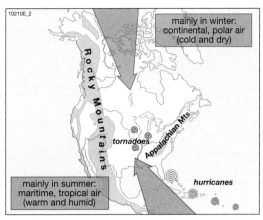

M4 Main air masses[18] in North America

Hurricanes

The wind speed in hurricanes is not as high as in tornadoes, but the destruction[12] is much greater. Hurricanes are about 150 miles in diameter[13] and wind speeds reach 150 mph. They get their enormous energy from rising warm, water-saturated[14] air coming from the tropical Atlantic Ocean. A hurricane spins[15] anti-clockwise and gains[16] even more energy as more humid warm air is drawn in from the ocean. All this energy is released as violent wind, which can cause enormous damage (M1) and, in the case of hurricane 'Katrina', led to flooding, when dykes[17] were destroyed (M5). During 'Katrina' nearly 1400 people died.

Tasks

1. Describe the damage shown in the photos (M1, M5).

2. What do blizzards, tornadoes, and hurricanes have in common?

3. Choose one storm type and find out more information using the Internet. Present your findings in English or in German.

Key terms:
- blizzard
- hurricane
- norther
- tornado/twister

pp. 8–9
Photographs

Helpful words and phrases
(for Task 1):
The photograph
... illustrates ...
... shows ...
... tells me...
... focuses on ...

(for Task 2):
Violent storms lead to ...
Extreme high winds ...
... can cause heavy precipitation ...
... may result in flooding, property damage, injuries, death, total destruction, loss of ...

---

[8] run (to) – *verlaufen*
[9] standstill – *Stillstand*
[10] suction – *Saugwirkung*
[11] on average – *durchschnittlich*
[12] destruction – *Zerstörung*
[13] in diameter – *im Durchmesser*
[14] saturated – *gesättigt*
[15] spin (to) – *drehen*
[16] gain (to) – *erhalten*
[17] dyke – *Deich*
[18] air mass – *Luftmassen*

DG_M1–010
www.diercke.com

The US Population – Melting Pot or Salad Bowl?

The USA, as it is today, was built by people who came from different countries. The Native[1] Americans, who are the American Indians and the Inuit, were forced[2] to move to reservations because white immigrants[3] claimed their homelands to settle there.

Until 1820, most of these people had come from England and the Netherlands. Between 1820 and 1860 many Irish people immigrated because there was great poverty[4] and hunger in Ireland. At the same time numerous[5] Germans moved there for political and religious reasons. In the 1880s over half a million Italians arrived in New York alone.

Blacks (African Americans), were brought into southern North America as slaves in the 17th and 18th century, and migrated[6] north in search for jobs.

In the second half of the 20th century many people came from Asian countries such as South Korea, Vietnam, and China.

Recently most immigrants came from Latin America. All immigrants from a Spanish-speaking background are called Hispanics.

M1 White

M2 Hispanic

M3 Black

M4 Asian

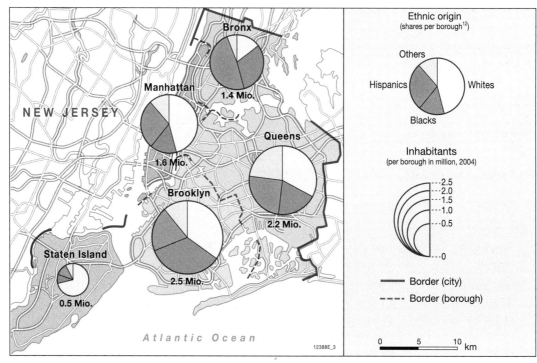

M5 Ethnic segregation in New York City (2004)

[1] native – *Ureinwohner, Eingeborener*
[2] force (to) – *zwingen*
[3] immigrant – *Einwanderer*
[4] poverty – *Armut*
[5] numerous – *zahlreich*

[6] migrate (to) – *wandern*
[7] custom – *Brauch, Sitte*
[8] ethnic segregation – *ethnische Trennung*
[9] ethnic integration – *ethnische Eingliederung*

Segregation and integration

Immigrants often want to live near people from the same country who speak the same language and have the same customs[7]. So, in New York and other cities you find blocks of houses where most people come from the same country. This is called ethnic segregation[8].

You can see ethnic segregation in New York City (M5), even though many of these ethnic groups have lived in America now for generations. This ethnic segregation is sometimes compared to a salad bowl because the bits of salad do not mix either.

On the other hand, ethnic integration[9] takes place. But even if they mix, for statistical reasons, people are asked to decide to which of the five major groups they belong. Anyway, it is very unlikely that the American population will ever become an ethnic melting pot[10]. In cities like New York you can observe social segregation, too. It means that people with the same income and similar jobs live close to each other in neighbourhoods[11]. M8 shows one way in which social segregation of poor people can be explained. The results are slums. Neighbourhoods like these are often called ghettos.

Helpful words and phrases:

(for Task1):

... The highest/ lowest percentage of ...

... a quarter (25 %) of ...

... half (50 %) of ...

... less/more than ...

... around/about ...

M6 Native American

M7 Afro-Asian

Poorer people move into the area ⬇   Wealthier[14] people move away from the area ⬆

Low income, little money — Low rents — Poor-quality housing — Little money from the government — Poor schools, bad education — Un-skilled jobs[17] — Unemployment[15], crime, drug abuse[16]

Social segregation of poor people

12209E_1

M8 Vicious cycle[13] leading to a slum

Helpful words and phrases

(for Task 3):

The flow chart...

... shows ...

... illustrates ...

... due to ...

... because of ...

... this leads to ...

... as a result ...

... as a consequence ...

| | 1980 | | 2000 | | 2020 | | 2040 | |
	(million)	(per cent)	(million)	(per cent)	(million)	(per cent)	(million)	(per cent)
White	180.9	79.9	196.7	71.6	206.2	63.9	205.6	56.4
Blacks	26.1	11.5	33.8	12.3	42.9	13.3	52.3	14.4
Hispanics	14.6	6.4	30.6	11.1	49.0	15.2	69.8	19.1
Asians	3.6	1.6	11.6	4.2	21.8	6.7	33.1	9.1
Native Americans	1.3	0.6	2.1	0.8	2.8	0.9	3.6	1.0
Total	226.5	100.0	274.8	100.0	322.6	100.0	364.3	100.0

M9 Population development in the USA 1980–2040 (2020 and 2040: estimates)

Key terms:
- American Indians
- Blacks (African Americans)
- integration/seg- regation (ethnic)
- ghetto
- Hispanics
- immigrant
- Inuit
- Native Americans
- slum
- segregation (social)
- Whites

Tasks

1 Describe the ethnic segregation in two boroughs of New York City (M5).

2 Suggest a method to turn M9 into a graphic. Give reasons for your decision.

3 Prepare a short speech in English or in German explaining M8.

pp. 20–21 Pie Charts

pp. 16–17 Bar Charts

pp. 12–13 Tables

[10] melting pot – *Schmelztiegel*
[11] neighbourhood – *Nachbarschaft*
[12] borough – *Stadtbezirk*
[13] vicious cycle – *Teufelskreis*

[14] wealthy – *wohlhabend*
[15] unemployment – *Arbeitslosigkeit*
[16] drug abuse – *Drogenmissbrauch*
[17] unskilled job – *ungelernte Tätigkeit*

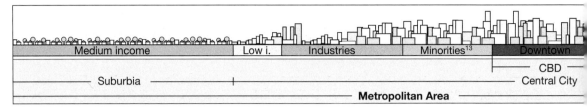

| Medium income | Low i. | Industries | Minorities[13] | Downtown |

CBD
Central City

Suburbia

Metropolitan Area

M1 Model profile of the US-American city

M2 Street pattern in San Francisco/CA

M3 CBD and industry in Cleveland/OH

M4 Residential area in Boston/MA

M5 Ghetto in the Bronx, New York City/NY

The US-American City

In all American cities you find a rectangular[1] pattern of roads, which is always a sign of central planning. In New York, Manhattan, for example, the 'Streets' run from northwest to southeast crossing the 'Avenues' which run from northeast to southwest at a right angle. This way blocks of houses are created (M2).

The central city

It is typical of all major cities in the USA to have a city centre (AE: downtown) with many skyscrapers[2]. In contrast to most European cities there is no old town centre. Most of the skyscrapers are in the Central Business District[3] (CBD), which is the centre of administration[4], shopping, business and entertainment.

Near the city centre, you often find secondary industries[5] (M3). Some of the residential areas[6] around the CBD have brick buildings from the early 20th century (M4). However, in several of these neighbourhoods the housing conditions[7] are quite bad. Only very poor people live in these slums (M5).

Suburbia

Many people with a higher income move away from the city to the suburbs[8], which stretch as far as 70 kilometres away from the city centre. These people are willing to commute[9] for several hours every day to and from work. Most of them use their cars, blocking the major roads into the cities. As a result many companies decide to move their factories and offices to the outskirts[10], too. Shops supply the ever-growing population. Schools and hospitals follow. Shopping centres (AE: malls) attract many customers and are important

---

[1] rectangular – *rechteckig*
[2] skyscraper – *Wolkenkratzer*
[3] Central Business District – *Hauptgeschäftsviertel*
[4] administration – *Verwaltung*
[5] secondary industries – *verarbeitende Industrie*

[6] residential area – *Wohngegend*
[7] housing conditions – *Wohnverhältnisse*
[8] suburb – *Vorort*
[9] commute (to) – *pendeln*
[10] outskirts – *Stadtrand*

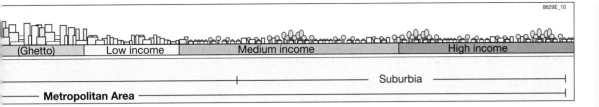

| (Ghetto) | Low income | Medium income | High income |

Suburbia

Metropolitan Area

8629E_10

meeting points for the people of suburbia[11]. Commuting to the central city becomes less important. Over the years the cities have been spreading more and more into the country-side. Geographers call it urban sprawl[12].

Gentrification

Over the last few decades, many of the old blocks near the CBD have been renovated and turned into expensive residential areas. So mostly wealthy people started to move back into the city centres in a process called gen-trification.

M6 Suburbs of Las Vegas/NV

Year	City	Metropolitan area
1950	3,620,962	4,945,000
1960	3,550,404	5,977,000
1970	3,366,957	6,716,000
1980	3,005,072	6,780,000
1990	2,783,726	6,792,000
2000	2,896,016	6,951,000
2004	2,862,244	7,065,000
2008	2.853.114	9.745.673

M7 Population development of Chicago/IL

M8 Mall in Minneapolis/MI

Key terms:

- administration
- CBD
- gentrification
- ghetto
- mall
- metropolitan area
- residential area
- shopping centre
- suburb
- suburbia
- outskirts
- urban sprawl

Tasks

1. Locate the cities from M2–M8 in your atlas.

2. Describe where in the profile M1 the photos are to be located.

3. Draw a line graph from the data in M7.

4. Describe and explain the population development in and around Chicago (M7) with the help of the text.

Helpful words and phrases (for Task 2):

The photo shows ...

...very high houses / build-ings / skyscrapers.

... industrial buildings.

... row of 2 to 3 storeyed houses / terraced build-ings.

... run down / demolished buildings.

Because of the ...
skyline,
appearance,
height of the buildings ...

The photo can be located in the . . . of the profile.

Helpful words and phrases (for Task 4):

The figures for ... grow to, rise to ...

The development ... continues ...

... stays the same

... sinks, falls, decreases to...

... varies between ...

pp. 14–15
Line Graphs

pp. 12–13
Tables

---

[11] suburbia – *Stadtumland*
[12] urban sprawl – *Zersiedlung*
[13] minority – *Minderheit*

DG_M1–014
www.diercke.com

M1 Cattle in a feedlot [1]/CO

Feedlots – Hotels for Beef Cattle?

Cattle ranching [2] is not about cowboys anymore. Only one per cent of the cattle in America are allowed to graze [3] on the prairies. Most of them spend the last half year of their 15-month life in feedlots. This is a form of intensive livestock farming [4], even in winter.

Cattle ranching is the biggest agricultural business in the USA. Calves [5] are born all year round on small and medium sized farms on the Great Plains, where they stay with their mother for the first six months. Bull calves will be castrated [6] soon after birth, so that their meat will taste as good as the meat of their sisters.

After being separated [7] from their mothers, still on the farm, the male steers [8] and female heifers [9] are trained to feed on protein- and fat-rich food. They have to learn this, because cows normally eat grass.

When they are nine months old, they are sent to feedlots, which can be up to one thousand kilometers away

There they are fattened up with a carefully designed daily mixture of 6.5 kg maize, 2.5 kg alfalfa [10] and 1 kg of a vitamin-protein-fat supplement [11], helped by implanted growth hormones.

All of this feed has to be transported to the feedlot and mixed up in the feed mill. The up to 100 000 animals in the feedlot are kept healthy by a daily dosis of antibiotics which is added in their drinking water, on average, 35 litres per day. After four to six months each animal weighs around 540 kg.

Most of the time, the steers and heifers are still owned by the farmer who pays a daily fee for feed and lodging, including the vet [12]: like full board [13] in a hotel.

When their time in the feedlot is up, the animals are transported by big trucks to a meat packing plant [14], where they are slaughtered, cut into pieces, which are then distributed to supermarkets and processing plants [15] throughout the country.

---

[1] feedlot – *Feedlot*
[2] cattle ranching – *Rinderhaltung*
[3] graze (to) – *grasen*
[4] intensive livestock farming – *Massentier-
haltung*
[5] calf – *Kalb*

[6] castrate (to) – *kastrieren*
[7] separate (to) – *trennen*
[8] steer – *Ochse*
[9] heifer – *Färse (junge Kuh)*
[10] alfalfa – *Luzerne*
[11] supplement – *Zusatz*

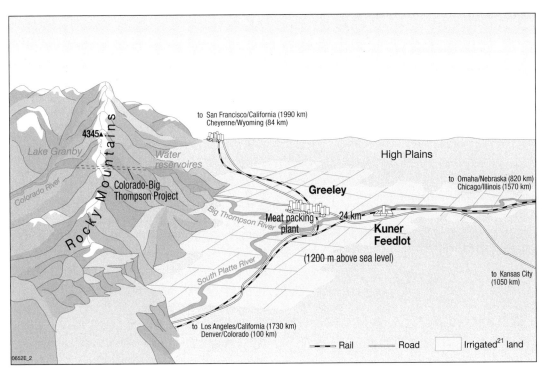

M2 Weld County/CO

Helpful words and phrases
(for Task 1):

The flow chart...
... shows ...
... illustrates ...
... helps us to understand ...
... is created by hand,
with a computer.

The starting point is ...

When we follow the arrows ...
This leads to ...
The output is ...

The end product/ the final result is ...

Feedlots have a huge impact[16] on the land use around them. Many farms produce feed for the feedlot, e.g. Maize or other crops (M2, M3).

Using the best seeds, often GM[17] maize, applying[18] pesticides and irrigating the fields might be very costly but will increase the yield. Artificial fertilizers[19] are often not needed as the farmers can use the liquid manure[20] from the feedlot itself.

Tasks

1 Turn the information about intensive livestock farming into a flow chart with the feedlot at its centre. Present your solution to the class.

2 Give a short talk about the life of a steer.

3 Calculate the daily amount of feed and water which are needed in a feedlot with 100 000 animals.

4 For experts: Do Internet research about the problems connected with intensive cattle ranching.

Key terms:
– cattle ranching
– feedlot
– fertilizer
– intensive livestock farming
– processing plant

pp. 22–23
Flow charts

pp. 24–25
Texts

pp. 36–37
Internet

pp. 20–21
Pie Charts

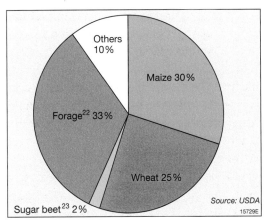

M3 Land use around the Kuner Feedlot (2007)

[12] vet (veterinarian) – *Tierarzt*
[13] full board – *Vollpension*
[14] meat packing plant – *Schlachthof*
[15] processing plant – *Verarbeitender Ind.-betrieb*
[16] impact – *Einfluss*
[17] GM (genetically modified) – *gentechnisch verändert*
[18] apply (to) – *verwenden*
[19] artificial fertilizer – *Kunst- / Chemiedünger*
[20] liquid manure – *Gülle*
[21] irrigate (to) – *bewässern*
[22] forage – *Grünfutter*
[23] sugar beet – *Zuckerrübe*

DG_M1–016
www.diercke.com

M1 Planting tomatoes with the help of GPS

M2 Drip irrigation in a tomato field

M3 A fully automated tomato harvester

M4 On the way to becoming ketchup

Modern Arable Farming[1]

Farming for ketchup

People in the USA eat more than 250 million litres of ketchup every year. The world's largest tomato-growing region lies in the USA, in Central Valley in California, which has ideal natural conditions for agriculture.

Only five per cent of the tomatoes are marketed[2] freshly, the others are processed and turned into salsa sauce, paste, pulp[3], tinned[4] tomatoes, or ketchup. All the well-known brands[5] have processing plants in California. Some of these companies own huge farms or have contracts[6] with local farmers, who grow the tomatoes on their farmland. Then the farmers sell the tomatoes to the food industry for a price which had been fixed before the tomatoes were even planted.

From March onwards the seedlings[7] are planted. On many farms the entire growing season is monitored[8] by satellite with the global positioning system (GPS)[9]. This high-tech system, together with the farming machinery, finds the right position for the seedlings near the drip irrigation[10] pipes. Computer technology helps to put the right amount of fertilizer or pesticide on the fields and it helps to keep records of where the yield was highest. So the farmer can use water, fertilizer, and pesticides even more efficiently in the following season, saving money and reducing the impact on the environment[11]. This type of agribusiness needs large fields to be profitable. During the planting and the harvesting season the farmers need extra help. Migrant workers, many of them illegal Hispanic immigrants from Mexico, find poorly-paid work on farms for only a few weeks in spring and in autumn.

As soon as the tomatoes are harvested, they are processed, filled in bottles, tins, and tubes, or used as ingredients for ready-to-eat meals[12]. Fresh tomatoes are transported by trucks throughout the United States.

[1] arable farming – *Ackerbau*
[2] market (to) – *vermarkten*
[3] pulp – *hier: Tomatenmark*
[4] tinned – *in Dosen*
[5] brand – *Marke*

[6] contract – *Vertrag*
[7] seedling – *Setzling*
[8] monitor (to) – *überwachen*
[9] Global Positioning System – *Globales Ortungssystem*

The best farmers in the world?

Today, agriculture in the USA is one of the most productive in the world (M6, M7). A large share of the production is exported, especially to countries in the developing world. The Great Plains in the Midwest of the United States are sometimes called the 'Breadbasket of the World', as ten per cent of the world's wheat is produced there.

In order to produce this amount[13] of food, most US farmers have turned their farms into agribusinesses which rely on[14] three factors:

– monoculture[15] – which means that they specialize mainly in one product,
– mechanization[16] – which means that they use a lot of machinery,
– chemicals – which are mainly pesticides and fertilizers.

Scientists[17] help the farmers to increase their yield, for example, with GM crops[18], with computer and satellite technology, or with new methods to save water. This is all very costly, and has led and is still leading to great changes in US agriculture.

However, food prices in the USA are among the lowest in the world: Americans spend ten per cent of their income on food (Germans 21 per cent). Nonetheless, the natural conditions such as relief, temperature, and precipitation play a very important role for the farmer. Although American farmers heavily depend[19] on export, production of GM foods sometimes creates[20] problems for them to export their goods.

Tasks

1. Use your atlas and M5 to explain why the natural conditions of Central Valley favour agriculture.

2. 'The US agriculture is one of the most productive in the world.' Explain.

3. Project: Find out and discuss the pros and cons of GM food in English or in German.

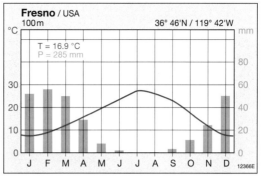

M5 Climate graph of Central Valley/CA

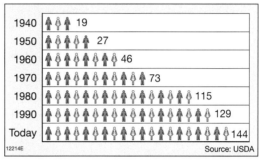

M6 Number of people fed by one US farmer

Product	Share of USA in world production	World rank
Maize	41 %	1
Soybeans	40 %	1
Cheese	28 %	1
Chicken	23 %	1
Beef	19 %	1
Oranges	14 %	1
Lettuce	22 %	2
Cotton[21]	19 %	2
Cereal[22]	16 %	2
Compare:		
Population	4.6 %	3
Area	6.5 %	3

M7 US farming in the world (2005)

Key terms:
– agribusiness
– arable farming
– drip irrigation
– fertilizer
– GM crops
– GPS
– mechanization
– migrant workers
– monoculture
– pesticide

Helpful words and phrases (for Task 1):

The maximum / minimum temperature is …

The driest / wettest month is …

The average annual temperature / precipitation is …

Because …

As a result …

When … then …

pp. 18–19 Climate Graphs

Hinweise für M7:
[21] cotton – *Baumwolle*
[22] cereal – *Getreide*

Helpful words and phrases (for Task 3):

… Firstly, next, after this …

… As you can see, let me show you …

… This brings me to, let's go back to …

… To sum up, in conclusion …

pp. 26–27 Prepare and Give a Talk

---

[10] drip irrigation – *Tröpfchenbewässerung*
[11] environment – *Umwelt*
[12] ready-to-eat-meal – *Fertiggericht*
[13] amount – *Menge*
[14] rely on (to) – *sich stützen auf*
[15] monoculture – *Monokultur*

[16] mechanization – *Mechanisierung*
[17] scientist – *Wissenschaftler*
[18] crop – *Anbaupflanze*
[19] depend on (to) – *abhängig sein von*
[20] create (to) – *schaffen*

DG_M1–018
www.diercke.com

From the Manufacturing Belt to the 'Rust Belt'

Hinweise für M2:

[20] coke
  – *Kohle*

[21] iron ore
  – *Eisenerz*

[22] limestone
  – *Kalkstein*

[23] blast furnace
  – *Hochofen*

[24] pig iron
  – *Roheisen*

[25] slag
  – *Schlacke*

[26] steel works
  – *Stahlwerk*

[27] foundry
  – *Gießerei*

[28] steel mill
  – *Walzwerk*

[29] pipes
  – *Rohre*

[30] wire
  – *Draht*

[31] steel plates
  – *Stahlblech*

M1 Iron- and steel-producing industry in Wisconsin

M2 Steel production

The beginning

At the beginning of industrialisation in the 19th century, iron and steel were the basic materials to manufacture[1] machines, trains, railway tracks, electric cables, ships, and household goods.

The Manufacturing Belt in the North-East of the United States offered ideal conditions for the iron and steel industry[2]. The raw materials[3] which were needed for the production of iron and steel were found not far from there: iron ore and limestone near the Great Lakes and coal to make coke in the Appalachian Mountains. Many workers lived in this area, because many immigrants from Europe had settled near the East Coast.

Metal industries[4] began to develop close to the steel mills in which more and more people found work. Steel was much needed all over North America. The growing population created a profitable market for all products.

> Well-known Belts in the USA are: the 'Wheat Belt', where a lot of wheat is grown, the 'Sunbelt' where the sun shines a lot, the 'Manufacturing Belt', where iron and steel is produced, and the 'Rust Belt', the new name for the declining Manufacturing Belt.

The period of growth

In 1908 Henry Ford from Detroit in the centre of the Manufacturing Belt started to produce the first car on an assembly line[5]: the Ford T4. It was a great success. Other car companies followed because cars became more and more popular around the world. So even more workers were needed and the car companies paid well. Supply industries[6] which produced, for example, tyres or brakes, settled nearby. The North-East became quite rich and Detroit became 'The Motor City'. The three most important car companies in the world, Ford, General Motors, and Chrysler, had their headquarters there. The car industry became the key industry[7] of the Manufacturing Belt.

The decline[8]

Since the 1970s people have started to move away from the North-East to other parts of the USA. Because of automation[9] less and less workers were needed in the car industry. The demand for American steel decreased. Japanese and European cars entered the US market successfully. Cars and their components[10] could be produced more cheaply in other countries, for example, in Mexico. So many steel mills lost their business and had to close. Without jobs, more and more people left the area. The Manufacturing Belt became known as the 'Rust Belt' (M1, M3).

---

[1] manufacture (to) – *herstellen*
[2] iron and steel industry – *Eisen- und Stahlindustrie*
[3] raw material – *Rohstoff*
[4] metal industry – *Metallindustrie*
[5] assembly line – *Fließband*

[6] supply industry – *Zulieferindustrie*
[7] key industry – *Schlüsselindustrie*
[8] decline – *Niedergang*
[9] automation – *Automatisierung*
[10] components – *Hier: Autoteile*

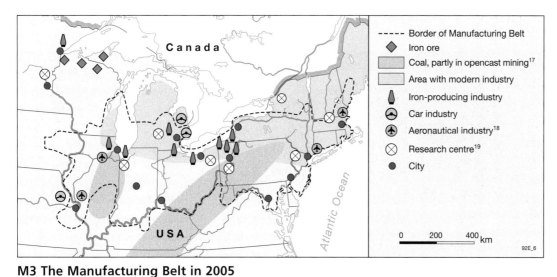

M3 The Manufacturing Belt in 2005

Legend:
- - - - Border of Manufacturing Belt
◆ Iron ore
▨ Coal, partly in opencast mining[17]
▢ Area with modern industry
⛏ Iron-producing industry
Ⓐ Car industry
✈ Aeronautical industry[18]
⊗ Research centre[19]
● City

0 200 400 km

92E_6

M4 Old cargo ships in front of new buildings in Pittsburgh/PA

The revival [11]

One third of all Americans still live in the Manufacturing Belt and many of them are qualified workers. It is the most densely populated part of the USA. To replace jobs which were lost in the manufacturing industry in the North-East, structural change [12] was needed. Growth industries [13] such as the aeronautical or the pharmaceutical [14] industry were set up near research centres, which were partly financed by the industry and partly by universities. Several top universities lie in the Manufacturing Belt. Harvard University and the Massachusetts Institute of Technology are ranked 1 and 2 in the world. They are both in the Boston area. So the North-East is an interesting region as a location [15] for modern industries. New jobs are created, many of them in R & D (research and development) [16].

Key terms:
- automation
- growth industry
- industrialisation
- iron- and steel-producing industry
- key industry
- location

- Manufacturing Belt
- manufacturing industry
- raw material
- research and development (R & D)
- structural change

Tasks

1 Work with the atlas and M3: Name the states and big cities which lie in the Manufacturing Belt.

2 Tell your classmates (in English and German) how steel is produced and processed (M2).

3 Describe and explain the development in the Manufacturing Belt.

pp. 6–7
Thematic Maps

Helpful words and phrases
(for Task 2):
Firstly, secondly, thirdly ...
The process begins, starts, continues with ...
After that, the next, last, final step ...,
The process ends with ...
There are several raw materials needed ...
Raw materials are transported, shipped, stored, mixed, added ...
Semi products / final products are processed, sold ...

pp. 24–25
Texts

---

[11] revival – *Wiederbelebung*
[12] structural change – *Strukturwandel*
[13] growth industry – *Wachstumsindustrie*
[14] pharmaceutical – *pharmazeutisch*
[15] location – *Standort*

[16] R & D – *Forschung und Entwicklung*
[17] opencast mining – *Tagebau*
[18] aeronautical industry – *Flugzeug- und Raumfahrtindustrie*
[19] research centre – *Forschungszentrum*

20 Topical Page

The Sunbelt – Combining Jobs with Pleasure

M1 Southern California in winter

Since the 1970s more and more industries have moved away from the Manufacturing Belt in the North-East and Midwest. First they moved to the West, first to California and later to the South-West, to Nevada, Arizona, New Mexico, and Texas. At the same time other industries started to grow in Louisiana, Mississippi, Alabama, Georgia and Florida.

These industries moved there for several reasons: Cheap land was available[1], the states' taxes[2] and the workers' wages[3] were low. There was a dense network[4] of roads and railways to transport components[5] and finished products[6] easily to other parts of the United States and abroad.

Skilled workers[7] moved there from the North-East because they could find work in the new industries, life was cheaper there, and the climate was pleasant as there was a lot of sunshine and often little rainfall per year. Because of this and because of the foot-loose industries, which settled there, this region became known as the Sunbelt.

Silicon Valley in California, south of San Francisco, is a well-known example in the Sunbelt as it has become the centre of the American computer industry (M4). All the famous hardware and software companies have got their offices there. They work

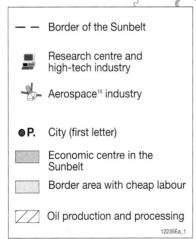

Legend:
- – – Border of the Sunbelt
- Research centre and high-tech industry
- Aerospace[16] industry
- ● **P.** City (first letter)
- Economic centre in the Sunbelt
- Border area with cheap labour
- Oil production and processing

12235Ea_1

M2 The Sunbelt

State	Per cent
Nevada	32.3
Arizona	28.6
Utah	24.7
Georgia	20.1
Idaho	19.5
Texas	18.9
Florida	16.0

Source: US Census Bureau

M3 Fastest growing states (population change 2000 – 2009

[1] available – *vorhanden*
[2] taxes – *Steuern*
[3] wages – *Löhne*
[4] dense network – *dichtes Netz von*
[5] components – *Teile, Zubehör*
[6] finished product – *Endprodukt*
[7] skilled worker – *gelernter Abeiter, Facharbeiter*
[8] rival – *Konkurrent*
[9] locational advantage – *Standortvorteil*

together with Stanford University and although they are rivals[8], they exchange their knowledge and the latest technologies quickly. This is an advantage for everyone and geographers call it locational advantage[9]. Though many industries have since moved away from Silicon Valley to cheaper production sites[10] abroad, the knowhow and cooperation[11] is still an advantage for the companies which stay there. The area near the Mexican border (M2), however, has attracted[12] a lot of unskilled workers[13]. Many of them are illegal immigrants[14] who hope to find work there.

Footloose industries
... are manufacturing industries which have a relatively free choice of location, because they do not depend on bulky raw materials[15]. The components and the finished products of these industries are light and easy to transport.

Key terms:
- components
- finished product
- footloose industries
- hi-tech industry
- locational advantage
- Sunbelt

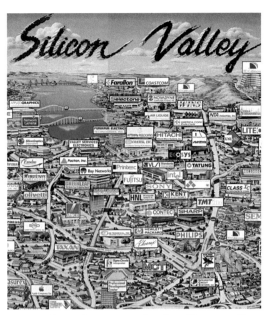

M4 High-tech companies in Silicon Valley

Helpful words and phrases
(for Tasks 1, 2):
something
- leads to ...
- causes ...
- starts ...
- results in ...
- has got a positive / negative effect on ...
- blocks ...
- ends ...

Tasks

1 List reasons why industries and people moved and still move to the Sunbelt.

2 Explain the growth of the states mentioned in M3. Use your atlas, too.

3 Explain the term Sunbelt in German. The text should have about 130 words.

pp. 24–25
Texts

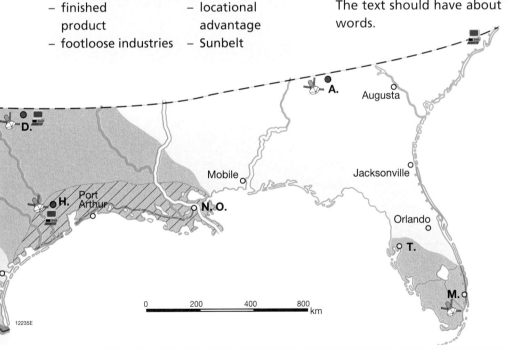

Augusta

Mobile

Jacksonville

Port Arthur
H.

N.O.

Orlando

T.

M.

A.

D.

0   200   400   800 km

12235E

---

[10] production site – *Produktionsstandort*
[11] cooperation – *Zusammenarbeit*
[12] attract (to) – hier: *anziehen (z. B. Arbeitsplätze)*
[13] unskilled worker – *ungelernter Arbeiter*

[14] illegal immigrant – *illegaler Einwanderer*
[15] bulky raw materials – *Massengüter (Rohstoffe)*
[16] aerospace – *Luft- und Raumfahrt*

Relief and Climate in the American West

1 Find the places given in the cross section in the atlas.

2 Fill in the height of precipitation at the locations given in M1 (see example for Colorado Springs).

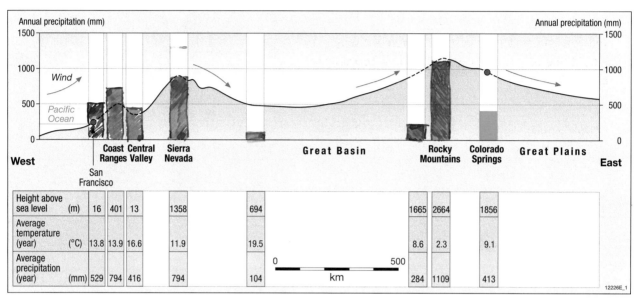

		Coast Ranges	Central Valley		Sierra Nevada		Great Basin		Rocky Mountains	Colorado Springs		Great Plains	
Height above sea level (m)		16	401	13	1358		694		1665	2664		1856	
Average temperature (year) (°C)		13.8	13.9	16.6	11.9		19.5		8.6	2.3		9.1	
Average precipitation (year) (mm)		529	794	416	794		104		284	1109		413	

West ... San Francisco ... East

0 — 500 km

M1 Cross section through the American West

3 Describe the effect of the following factors on the temperature in the American West (M1):
a) height of place.
b) exposition[1] (windward side/leeward side).
c) distance from the Pacific Ocean.

4 Describe the role of the following factors on the precipitation in the American West (M1):
a) height of place.
b) exposition (windward side/leeward side).
c) distance from the Pacific Ocean.

Helpful words and phrases (for Tasks 3, 4):
The higher a place lies, the ..... it becomes.
On the wind-ward side it is ... whereas on the leeward side it is ...
The nearer you are to the Pacific Ocean the ... it is, the farther away you are from the Pacific Ocean, the ... it becomes.

_____

_____

_____

_____

_____

_____

5 For experts: Do research on the connection between height, temperature, and precipitation: Present a 1 minute article for a podcast (sound-file).

[1] exposition – *Ausrichtung (zu Sonne und Wind)*

A Tabular[1] View of the Contrasting Nature of Northern America

1 To describe the natural conditions in the different parts of North America, complete the table with the help of the information given in the text (page 4/5) and in the atlas.

2 Tell your classmates in a short statement why you would like or would dislike living in a certain part of Northern America.

Helpful words and phrases (for Task 1):
mostly, mainly, largely, on the whole, in general, …
a huge (most of the) area is covered by, …

pp. 4–7 Physical/Thematic Maps

[1] tabular – *tabellarisch*

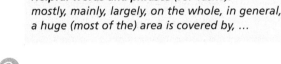

Region	North	East	South	West	Centre
US States as examples	(Canada) Alaska	(Delaware) USA	(Texas) USA	(California) (USA)	(South Dakota) (USA)
Relief	Rocky mountains, (Rockys)	Atlantic coastal plain, Appalachian Mts., Central Lowland	Atlantic coastal, ~~Flatter~~ Gulf of Mexico (coastal plain)	Pacific coast mountains Great Basin	centre north america mainly flat plains
Climate	Cold winters, cold summers, Subpolar climate temperate in south	moderate year round 10° warmer in winter und 10° cooler in summer (maritime climate)	Mild winters, hot summers, rain mainly in the summer or autumn	mediterrane in climate. hot summer. freezin temperatures are rare, even in winter.	continental climate cold dry winters, hot and semi-humid summers.
Vegetation	big forest and also aquatic vegetation tundra in the south.	trees include oak, hickory, maple... forest steppe	woody plants like Mesquine, greasewh. desert	Black cottonwood, white alder, California sycamore. desert	A huge area is covered by steppe (west) and deciduous forests (east)
Land use	Summerfallow land, Christmas tree area, natural land for pasture. Agriculture in protected area	intense agriculture, dairy farming	95% of land in texas is privately owned private land ranch or forest. cotton tabacco	Market gardening near coast, extensive cattle ranching elsewhere	Farms, Acres, Sugarbeat

'Don't Be Scared, Just Be Prepared'

DISASTER SUPPLY KIT

- **Water** – at least 1 gallon[1] daily per person for 3 to 7 days
- **Food** – at least enough for 3 to 7 days
  - non-perishable[2] packaged or canned food[3]/juices
  - foods for infants or the elderly
  - snack foods
  - non-electric can opener
  - cooking tools/fuel[4]
  - paper plates/plastic utensils
- **Blankets[5]/Pillows[6], etc.**
- **Clothing** – seasonal/rain gear/sturdy shoes
- **First Aid Kid/Medicines/Prescription Drugs[7]**
- **Special Items** – for babies and the elderly
- **Toiletries/Hygiene items/Moisture wipes[8]**
- **Flashlight/Batteries**
- **Radio** – Battery operated and NOAA[9] weather radio
- **Telephones** – Fully charged cell phone with extra battery and a traditional (not cordless) Telephone set

- **Cash (with some small bills) and Credit Cards**
  - Banks and ATMs[10] may not be available for extended periods
- **Keys**
- **Toys, Books and Games**
- **Important documents**
  - in a waterproof container or watertight resealable[11] plastic bag
  - insurance[12], medical records[13], bank account numbers, Social Security Card, etc.
- **Tools** – keep a set with you during the storm
- **Vehicle fuel tanks filled**
- **Pet care items**
  - identification/immunization records/medications
  - supply of food and water
  - a carrier or cage
  - muzzle[14] and leash[15]

Source:
http://www.nhc.noaa.gov/HAW2/english/prepare/supply_kit.shtml

M1 The leaflet from the National Hurricane Centre is useful to prepare for any disaster

1   List the items from M1 you and your family would take in case of an approaching hurricane. Give reasons.

_____

_____

_____

Helpful words and phrases:
Something is ... important, essential, necessary, vital, because ...
I would prefer to, I would not forget to, In my opinion, I think ...

[1] gallon – *3,8 Liter (USA)*
[2] non perishable – *unverderblich*
[3] canned food – *Konserve*
[4] fuel – *Brennstoff*
[5] blanket – *Decke*
[6] pillow – *Kopfkissen*

[7] prescription drug – *verschreibungspflichtiges Arzneimittel*
[8] moisture wipes – *Feuchttücher*
[9] NOAA – *U.S. Wetterdienst (National Oceanic and Atmosperic Administration)*
[10] ATM – *Geldautomat*

[11] resealable – *wiederverschließbar*
[12] insurance – *hier: Versicherungsunterlagen*
[13] medical record – *Behandlungsunterlage*
[14] muzzle – *Maulkorb*
[15] leash – *Leine*

Indicator	Census Area			Units
	112.02	168	116	
Population density	4615	20015	19861	Inh./sqkm
Whites	82.8	13.4	72.7	per cent
Hispanics	11.5	57.3	9.5	per cent
Blacks	0.8	25.5	2.9	per cent
Asians	4.9	3.8	14.9	per cent
Households income <10000 US-$	12.2	28.5	7.1	per cent
Adults w. < 9 years education	0.0	21.7	1.8	per cent
Average household income	546409	77105	68022	US-$/year

M1 Comparison of three census areas in Mid Manhattan

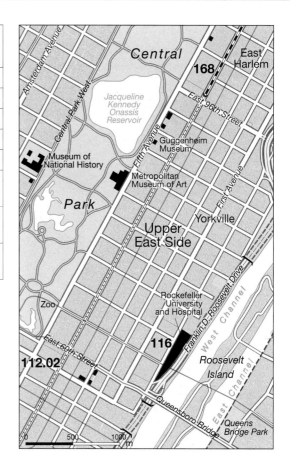

1 Turn the figures marked yellow into three pie charts. Afterwards write a short text about the ethnic segregation in Mid Manhattan.

2 With the help of the table and the map complete the text below. Some of the expressions can be found in the following list.

List: low, ethnic, highest, average household income, all adults have an education longer than nine years, Hispanic, high, quarter

pp. 20 – 21 Pie Charts

When we compare the three census areas, not only _____ segregation becomes visible.

You can see that the areas with the _____ population density have the lowest average household income.

In the census area _____ at the south-eastern tip of Central Park the conditions are much better:

The population density is _____ and the average household income is very _____ . The people there

seem to be well-educated because _____ .

You can see if people are well off, when the _____ is high and there are

only few households with an income of _____ . The census area where the most

poor people live is _____ because more than a quarter of the households earn less

than _____ per year, lies _____ . More than half the people there have

a _____ origin and a _____ of them are Blacks. The education standards are quite _____ ,

as more than a fifth of the adults here went _____ to school.

1 Use the key terms and the text from pages 12 - 13 to solve the crossword puzzle. Write two-word expressions as one word (example: residentialarea). Put the letters in the marked boxes in the right order to get the name of a US city named after an American president.

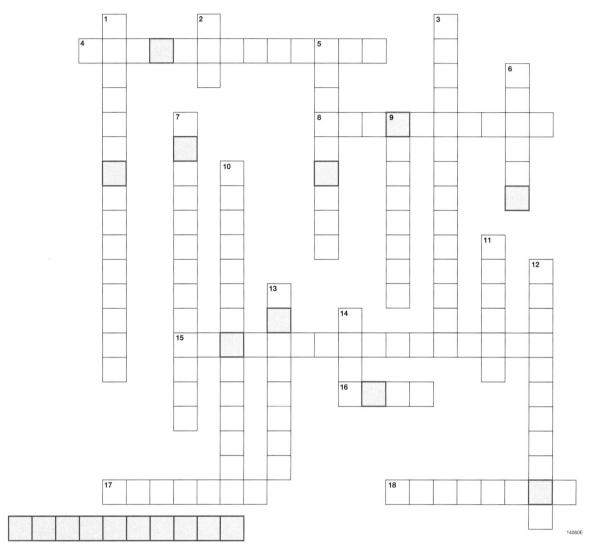

14060E

Waagerecht / Across

4. houses next to each other
8. a house so high that it touches the sky
15. region which includes one or more major cities
16. shopping area outside the CBD
17. the way people live
18. city centre (AE)

Senkrecht / Down

1. where the people live
2. where most skyscrapers are
3. rich people move back to the city centre
5. area further away from the city centre

6. segregated, mostly poor part of a city
7. one of the three main functions of the CBD
9. all suburbs together
10. in the CBD, the townhall is the centre of …
11. as far as 70 kilometres away from the city centre
12. unrestricted growth of the city into the countryside
13. most people go downtown for …
14. run-down residential area

The name of the city is

___ ___ ___ ___ ___ ___ ___ ___ ___ ___

1 Use the examples in the two horizontal bar charts to complete the charts by adding the missing data for 'Today' (crops) and for '1900' (livestock) from M1.

Farms with	Per cent	
Crop/Livestock	1900	Today
Maize	81	22
Wheat	37	13
Oats [1]	38	5
Barley [2]	7	4
Sorghum [3]	1	5
Soybeans [4]	0	18
Tobacco	8	6
Cotton [5]	24	2
Vegetables	61	3
Hay [6] / forage [7]	62	47
Orchards [8] (1929)	46	6
Chickens	96	6
Cattle (total)	82	44
– of which were/ are Milk cows	78	7
Pigs	76	6
Horses	79	19
Mules [9]	25	2

M1 Changes in US agriculture between 1900 and today

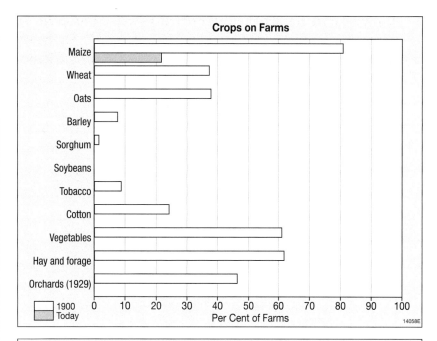

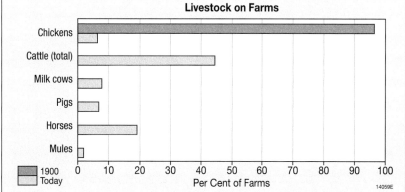

pp. 16–17 Bar Charts
pp. 26–27 Prepare and Give a Talk

2 Use the two completed charts to prepare a talk (in German or in English) about the specialization which has taken place in the American agriculture since 1900. Use the space below for notes.

_____

_____

_____

_____

_____

_____

[1] oats   –   *Hafer*
[2] barley   –   *Gerste*
[3] sorghum   –   *Hirse*
[4] soybean   –   *Sojabohne*
[5] cotton   –   *Baumwolle*

[6] hay   –   *Heu*
[7] forage   –   *Grünfutter*
[8] orchard   –   *Obstgarten*
[9] mule   –   *Maultier*

© *westermann*, Braunschweig

Changes in the Location of the American Car Industry

1 Name three important changes that have taken place in the US car industry after 1986 in three statements by comparing the maps (M1).

1. _less manu facters/less employess_

2. _More Foreign_ ~~cars~~ ~~manu~~

3. _More spaceed out_

2 Make a table in your exercise book showing the effects that these changes have had on the Manufacturing Belt. Use the text on page 18 and 19.

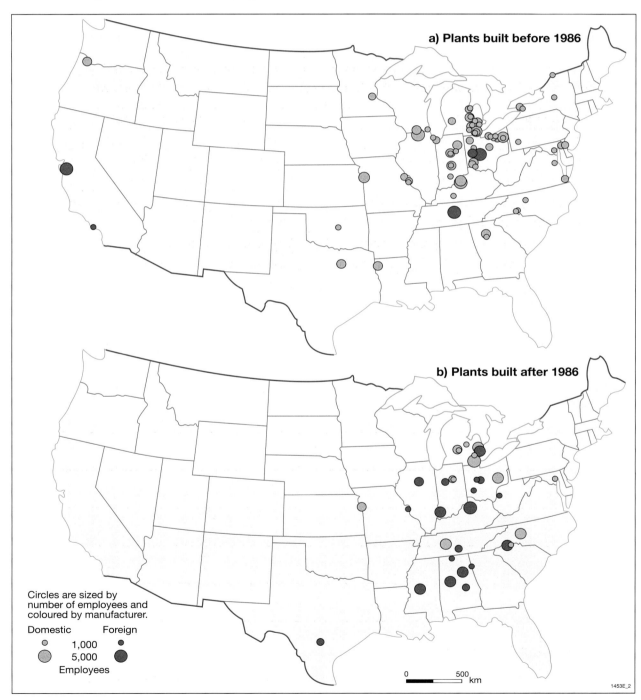

Circles are sized by number of employees and coloured by manufacturer.

Domestic   Foreign

○ 1,000 ●
○ 5,000 ●

Employees

0   500 km

1453E_2

M1 The location of the US car industry

Where Will the Computer Chips Manufacturer Settle?

Computer Chips

- *Where are computer chips used?*

Computer chips are everywhere, not only in computers. You find them in cars, telephones, TV sets, cameras, printers, traffic lights, lifts, credit cards, USB sticks, clocks, heating systems, etc. The most advanced[1] chips are microprocessors in computers.

- *Which raw materials are needed to produce computer chips?*

Silicon (which is made from sand), chemicals and gases, UV light, and some metals.

- *How are they made?*

Computer chips are produced by machines in absolutely[2] dust-free[3] rooms. Only a few workers are needed to control the expensive machines. Scientists develop and test new types of chips and programme them.

1 A manufacturer of computer chips is looking for a location for a new factory. Find the three most important reasons in this list, which will most probably influence his decision. Rank the three aspects.

Location at a sea port	Highly skilled workers available
Telephone network[4] available	Many unskilled workers for easy jobs available
Glassfibre cable network available	Companies producing high-tech articles are present
Easy access[5] to public transport[6]	Several computer chip producers are already there
Enough parking space for customers	Location close to an international airport
Huge car park for lorries	Clean environment[7]
Enough space for storing raw materials	Low price for building sites
Warm and sunny climate all year round	Easy access to motorways
Low taxes	No laws against pollution[8]
Support from the local government	Famous universities are nearby
Railway tracks to transport bulky goods	Many outdoor and indoor leisure facilities[9]
Raw materials nearby	New shops, schools and hospitals nearby

My three most important reasons for the new location of the computer chip factory are:

1. _____

because _____

2. _____

because _____

3. _____

because _____

[1] advanced – *hoch entwickelt*
[2] absolutely – *völlig*
[3] dust-free – *staubfrei*
[4] network – *Netz*
[5] access – *Zugang*
[6] public transport – *öffentliche Verkehrsmittel*
[7] clean environment – *saubere Umwelt*
[8] pollution – *Umweltverschmutzung*
[9] leisure facilities – *Freizeitstätten*

1 Find the fitting English expressions for the German definitions. You have to write a two-word expression as one word (example: residential area = residentialarea).

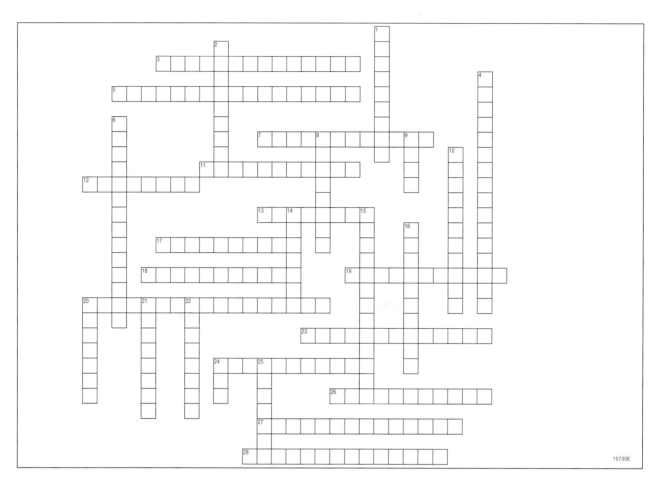

15730E

Waagerecht / Across

3. Niederschlag an Gebirgen
5. wichtigste Industrieregion der USA
7. moderner landwirtschaftlicher Großbetrieb
11. räumliche Trennung aufgrund sozialer Unterschiede
12. feuchtes Klima mit niedrigen Temperaturschwankungen
13. Einwohner der USA mit spanischsprachigen Wurzeln
17. Wasserzufuhr auf landwirtschaftlichen Anbauflächen
18. Beschränkung auf eine Anbaufrucht
19. wichtigstes Getreideanbaugebiet der USA
20. Industrie ohne zwingende Standortbindung
23. Ausstattung mit Maschinen
24. trockenes Klima mit hohen Temperaturschwankungen
26. wichtigste Industrie einer Region
27. Ausstattung mit Arbeitskraft ersetzenden Maschinen
28. größtes Gebirge der USA

Senkrecht / Down

1. tropischer Wirbelsturm in Nord- und Mittelamerika
2. Mittel zur Schädlingsbekämpfung
4. Modernisierung durch Ersetzung alter Industrien
6. Verdrängung angestammter Bewohner durch Wohlhabendere
8. Schneesturm
9. heruntergekommener Stadtteil
10. ungeordnete Ausbreitung einer Stadtregion
14. Industrieregion im Süden und Westen der USA
15. Hauptanbaugebiet Kaliforniens
16. zusätzliche Pflanzennährstoffe in der Landwirtschaft
20. Viehmast-Großbetrieb
21. Standort eines Industrie- oder Dienstleistungsbetriebes
22. Sammelbegriff für die Vorstädte
24. Abkürzung für das städtische Dienstleistungszentrum
25. kurzlebiger Wirbelsturm   © *westermann*, Braunschweig

Phonetic symbols

Vowels				Dipthongs		Consonants			
ɑː	arm	i	happy	aɪ	eye	ŋ	song	ð	these
ʌ	but	iː	easy	aʊ	our	r	red	θ	bathroom
e	desk	ɒ	orange	eə	air	s	sister	v	very
ə	an	ɔː	all	eɪ	take	z	zebra	w	what
ɜː	bird	ʊ	look	ɪə	here	ʒ	television		*Stress*
æ	apple	u	January	ɔɪ	boy	dʒ	sausage	'	Main stress in a word
ɪ	in	uː	boot	əʊ	go	ʃ	fresh	ˌ	Secondary stress in a word coming before the main stress.
				ʊə	your	tʃ	child		

 pp. 50–63
Glossary

administration [ədˌmɪnɪˈstreɪʃ(ə)n]
Verwaltung – Activities needed to manage the affairs of a government, a business, an organisation, etc.

agribusiness [ˈægrɪˌbɪznəs]
Agrobusiness – Farming on a large scale, often combining growth and marketing.

American Indians [əˈmerɪkən ˈɪndiəns]
Indianer – (amerikanische Ureinwohner)

arable farming [ˈærəb(ə)l ˈfɑː(r)mɪŋ]
Ackerbau – Growing of crops on farms.

automation [ˌɔːtəˈmeɪʃ(ə)n]
Automatisierung – Way of production which tries to replace workers by machines, e.g. robots.

basin [ˈbeɪs(ə)n]
Becken – Depression or low area on the land's surface.

Blacks (African Americans)
[blæks (ˈæfrɪkən əˈmerɪkəns)]
Schwarze (Afroamerikaner)

blizzard [ˈblɪzə(r)d]
Blizzard, Schneesturm

boreal [ˈbɔːriəl]
boreal (boreale Ökozone) – Referring to a rather cold climate with great differences between warm summers and cold winters, → *coniferous forests* are the typical vegetation.

cattle ranching [ˈkæt(ə)l ˈrɑːntʃɪŋ]
Rinderhaltung – Rearing of cattle.

CBD, Central Business District
[ˈsentrəl ˈbɪznəs ˈdɪstrɪkt]
Hauptgeschäftsviertel – Area of a city which is the centre of → *administration*, shopping, business, entertainment.

climate [ˈklaɪmət]
Klima – Average weather conditions of a certain region over at least 30 years.

climatic zone [ˈklaɪˈmætɪk zəʊn]
Klimazone – Area with a consistent → *climate*. → *Polar*, → *Temperate*, → *Subtropical*, and → *Tropical Zone*.

coastal plain [ˈkəʊst(ə)l pleɪn]
Küstenebene

component [kəmˈpəʊnənt]
Komponente, Teil, Zubehör

coniferous forest [kəˈnɪf(ə)rəs ˈfɒrɪst]
Nadelwald – Forest with trees having needle-shaped leaves.

continental climate
[ˌkɒntɪˈnent(ə)l ˈklaɪmət]
Kontinentalklima – Climate with high temperature range between warm summers and cold winters.

deciduous forest [dɪˈsɪdjuəs ˈfɒrɪst]
Laubwald – Forest with trees which shed leaves in winter.

desert [ˈdezə(r)t]
Wüste – Dry zone covered with rock, gravel or sand; only sparse vegetation.

drip irrigation [drɪp ˌɪrɪˈgeɪʃ(ə)n]
Tröpfchenbewässerung – Kind of watering plants in dry regions by drops of water coming from water pipes to provide plants with just the amount of water they need.

feedlot [ˈfiːdlɒt]
Feedlot (Form der Rinderhaltung)

fertilizer [ˈfɜː(r)təlaɪzə(r)]
Dünger – Substance (natural or chemical) which farmers add to the soil to help plants to grow better.

finished product [ˈfɪnɪʃt ˈprɒdʌkt]
Endprodukt

footloose industry [ˈfʊtˌluːs ˈɪndəstri]
standortneutrale Industrie – Industry where the location is not influenced strongly by access to → *raw materials* or markets.

gentrification [ˌdʒentrɪfɪˈkeɪʃ(ə)n]
Gentrifizierung – Movement of wealthy people mostly into inner cities after the renovation and restoration of the buildings and flats **often** combined with the out-migration of the former inhabitants.

ghetto [ˈgetəʊ]
Ghetto – Segregated area in a city where a minority lives; originally the residential concentration of Jews.

GM crops [ˌdʒiː ˈem krɒps]
gentechnisch veränderte Feldfrüchte

GPS, global positioning system
[ˈgləʊb(ə)l pəˈzɪʃ(ə)nɪŋ ˈsɪstəm]
Globales Ortungssystem

growth industry [grəʊθ ˈɪndəstri]
Wachstumsindustrie – Type of industry which produces products which are in great demand because they are innovative and modern and so lead to a further growth of that industry.

high-tech industry [haɪ tek ˈɪndəstri]
Hochtechnologie-Industrie – Industry using advanced skills and machines.

Hispanics [hɪˈspænɪks]
US-Bürger mit spanischem Sprachhintergrund

hurricane [ˈhʌrɪkən]
Hurrikan – System of strong winds circulating around a low-pressure area in Central and North America, combined with heavy rainfall and thunderstorms.

immigrant [ˈɪmɪgrənt]
Einwanderer

Inuit [ˈɪnuɪt] *Inuit*

iron and steel producing industry
[aɪə(r)n ænd stiːl prəˈdjuːsɪŋ ˈɪndəstri]
Eisen- und Stahlindustrie

industrialisation [ɪnˈdʌstriəlaɪˈzeɪʃ(ə)n]
Industrialisierung – Process of developing secondary industries in a country.

integration [ˌɪntɪˈgreɪʃ(ə)n]
Eingliederung – Process of bringing together different groups, regions, or countries to improve cooperation.

key industry [kiː ˈɪndəstri]
Schlüsselindustrie – Industry of primary importance to an economy, for example the car industry.

leeward side [ˈliːwə(r)d saɪd]
windabgewandte Seite – Side (mainly of a mountain) which faces away from the oncoming wind direction.

livestock farming
[ˈlaɪvˌstɒk ˈfɑː(r)mɪŋ]
Viehwirtschaft – Rearing of farm animals for the production of milk or meat.

location [ləʊˈkeɪʃ(ə)n]
Standort – Area or place for industries or businesses.

locational advantage
[ˌləʊkəlaɪˈzeɪʃ(ə)n(ə)l ədˈvɑːntɪdʒ]
Standortvorteile

lowlands ['ləʊləndz]
Tiefebene – Flat, low lying landscape.

manufacturing industry
[ˌmænjʊˈfæktʃərɪŋ ˈɪndəstri]
verarbeitende Industrie – Business of producing goods in factories.

manufacturing site
[ˌmænjʊˈfæktʃərɪŋ saɪt]
Produktionsstätte – Place or location where goods are produced in factories.

mall [mɔːl]
Einkaufszentrum (USA)

mangrove swamp ['mæŋˌgrəʊv swɒmp]
Mangrovensumpf – A coastal area in the Tropics influenced by the tides, where mangroves, tropical evergreen trees, grow.

Manufacturing Belt
[mænjʊˈfæktʃərɪŋ belt]
Industriegürtel im Nordosten der USA

maritime climate
['mærɪˌtaɪm ˈklaɪmət]
maritimes Klima – Climate with little temperature differences between cool summers and mild winters.

metropolitan area
[ˌmetrəˈpɒlɪt(ə)n ˈeəriə]
Ballungsraum – Very large urban settlement consisting of cities surrounded by urban areas with a total population exceeding 1,000,000 inhabitants.

mechanization [ˌmekənaɪˈzeɪʃ(ə)n]
Mechanisierung – Process in industrial production where manual work is replaced by machines.

migrant worker
['maɪgrənt ˈwɜː(r)kə(r)]
Gastarbeiter – Person who goes to live and work in another region or country.

monoculture ['mɒnəʊˌkʌltʃə(r)]
Monokultur – Cultivation of one main crop, usually on large fields.

Native American ['neɪtɪv əˈmerɪkən]
Ureinwohner Amerikas

norther ['nɔːðə]
US-Bezeichnung eines kalten Nordwinds

outskirts ['aʊtˌskɜː(r)ts]
Stadtrand – Areas at the edge of a town or city, far away from the centre.

pesticide ['pestɪsaɪd]
Pestizid – Chemical substance used in farming to kill insects.

plain [pleɪn]
Ebene

plateau ['plætəʊ]
Hochebene – Rather flat area which is higher above sea level than the surrounding land.

Polar Zone ['pəʊlə(r) zəʊn]
Polarzone – Zone between the Polar Circle and the pole.

precipitation [prɪˌsɪpɪˈteɪʃ(ə)n]
Niederschlag – Condensed water vapour from the atmosphere which reaches the surface of the earth.

processing plant ['prəʊsesɪŋ plɑːnt]
Verarbeitender Industriebetrieb

research and development, R & D
[rɪˈsɜː(r)tʃ ænd dɪˈveləpmənt]
Forschung und Entwicklung – Two closely related processes by which new products are created or old products are improved through technological innovation.

rain shadow [reɪn ˈʃædəʊ]
Regenschatten – Area on the → *leeward side* of a mountain, where there is little or no rainfall due to descending air masses.

raw material [rɔː məˈtɪəriəl]
Rohstoff – Unprocessed material used for the production of goods.

relief [rɪˈliːf]
Relief – Shape of the Earth's surface.

relief rainfall [rɪˈliːf ˈreɪnˌfɔːl]
Steigungsregen – Rainfall caused by rising air masses, which cool down due to mountain ranges. This leads to the condensation of water vapour and → *precipitation*.

residential area
[ˌrezɪdenʃ(ə)l ˈeəriə]
Wohngebiet – Area which is used for building private houses.

segregation [ˌsegrɪˈgeɪʃ(ə)n]
Segregation, Entmischung – Enforced distribution of specific groups of people into distinct areas, usually based on race, income or religion.

shopping centre ['ʃɒpɪŋ ˈsentə(r)]
Einkaufszentrum

slum [slʌm]
Armen-, Elendsviertel – housing area, usually in very big towns, which is in a bad condition and the home of mainly very poor people.

structural change
['strʌktʃ(ə)rəl tʃeɪndʒ]
Strukturwandel – Change in the socio-economic structure of an area over a longer period of time, e.g. after the decline of a major industry.

Subtropical Zone
[ˌsʌbˈtrɒpɪk(ə)l zəʊn]
Suptropische Zone – Zone between the Tropic of Cancer and 40°N, respectively between the Tropic of Capricorn and 40°S.

suburb ['sʌbɜː(r)b]
Vorort – → *Residential area* located at the → *outskirts* of a city.

suburbia [səˈbɜː(r)biə]
Stadtumland – → *Residential areas*, usually located at the border of a bigger city.

Sunbelt ['sʌnˌbelt]
Industriegürtel im Süden der USA

temperature ['temprɪtʃə(r)]
Temperatur

Temperate Zone
['temp(ə)rət zəʊn]
gemäßigte Zone – Zone between the → *Subtropical Zone* and the → *Polar Zone*, extending between about 40° and the Arctic Circle.

tornado [tɔː(r)ˈneɪdəʊ]
Wirbelsturm – Very destructive, short-lived, revolving storm, usually together with rain and thunder.

Tropical Zone ['trɒpɪk(ə)l zəʊn]
Tropische Zone – Zone between the Tropic of Cancer and the Tropic of Capricorn.

tundra ['tʌndrə]
Tundra – Polar and subpolar vegetation zone where short and cool summers and the permafrost soil only allow the growth of grass, moss, lichen and small bushes.

uplands ['ʌpləndz]
Hochland – High lying areas of the Earth, e.g. plains and → *basins* in mountainous regions or hilly and mountainous area with mountain heights under 1 500 m.

urban sprawl ['ɜː(r)bən sprɔːl]
Zersiedlung – Unrestricted or unregulated spread of → *urban areas*.

windward side ['wɪndwə(r)d saɪd]
windzugewandte Seite – Side which faces the oncoming wind.

Sources:

Corbis, Düsseldorf: Titel (Alan Copson/JAI), 11 M6 (SYGMA), 12 M3, 12 M4, 13 M6 (Lefkowitz), 14 M1 (Hamilton Smith); Geospace, Salzburg: 12 M2 (Beckel); Gerster, Georg, Zumikon: 5 M6; Getty Images, München: 8 M3 (Jupiterimages/International Stock); Huber, Bildagentur, Garmisch-Partenkirchen: 7 M6 (Gräfenhain); images.de, Berlin: 16 M4 (Photovault); mauritius images, Mittenwald: 7 M2, 7 M5 (imagebroker.net); Mittal Steel Company, Chicago: 18 M1; Nitzsche, Peter/RUTGERS New Jersey Agricultural Experiment Station: 16 M2; NOAA, Washington: 8 M1, 8 M2; Picture-Alliance, Frankfurt/M.: 4 M3 (Okapia), 5 M7 (epa Kleponis), 7 M3 (Castelein), 10 M1 (epa Bieri), 10 M2 (Hahn), 10 M3 (Photos hot/Band Photo), 10 M4 (Dietsch), 11 M7 (epa Campbell), 12 M5 (dpa), 13 M8 (Melchert), 20 M1 (Bildagentur Huber/Simeone); Pik Rite Inc., Lewisburg/PA: 16 M3; Rieke, Michael, Hannover: 7 M4; Strohbach, Dietrich, Berlin: 4 M2; University of California, Davis: 16 M1 (Upadhyaya); Woszczyna, M.: 19 M4; www.webport.com: 21 M4.